Mechanical Birds

Poems

Mechanical Birds

poems by

Denver Butson

St. Andrews College Press
Laurinburg, North Carolina
2000

This book made possible through the *Richard Walser and Bernice Kelley Harris Fund* of the Hanes Charitable Lead Trust

Copyright © 2000 by Denver Butson

Library of Congress Cataloging-in-Publication Data

Butson, Denver. Mechanical birds/Denver Butson—
Laurinburg, NC/St. Andrews College Press
I. Butson, Denver. II. Title

St. Andrews College Press
1700 Dogwood Mile
Laurinburg, NC 28352

www.sapc.edu/sapress

author photograph by Cedric N. Chatterley,
© 1999 Cedric N. Chatterley

cover detail from "Rooster Boy," oil on canvas,
1997 by Melissa Goodling.

The author wishes to thank—

The editors of *Cairn*, *LUNGFULL*, and *Ikons*, in which a number of these poems have appeared in sometimes slightly different versions;

and Agha Shahid Ali, Ron Bayes, Michael Carroll, Cedric N. Chatterley, Pete Dulgar, Melissa Goodling, Greg Hershey, Rhonda Keyser, Andrew Miller, Jesse Nissim and Edmund White for their help with this book;

and Janet Lefever Butson and Joseph Butson for putting up with the "My Mother/My Father" poems.

Praise for *triptych*
(The Commoner Press, 1999)

"Original, necessary, and musical"
—Ned Rorem.

"Seldom do I read a book with such admiration and am struck by such energy and ingenuity."
—Thom Gunn

"Denver Butson's work is splendid and quite remote from the MFA-sodden factories."
—Jim Harrison

"Denver Butson's poetry may remind us in places of the fables and stories of Russell Edson, but there is more, and what is more is undeniably Denver's. If a man is on fire, a woman is drowning, and another is freezing as all three stand at the bus stop, it reveals something of the entirety of the human condition, as seen and acted upon by Denver. The result is a thoroughly satisfying experience for an engaged reader. Bravo."
—Theodore Enslin

"Subtle and evocative language."
— W.S. Merwin

"Denver Butson writes of crows and drownings, hands of lovers and hands of clocks, moving all things with an equal and passionate intensity."
—Elena Alexander

"There are almost as many surprises in Denver Butson's triptych as there are in Magritte's paintings. When this poet disturbs the words, he brings baffled joy one minute and an acute sense of menace the next. Yet Denver Butson knows, just as well, when to leave an image stark, serious: something we cannot avoid: something we have to fill for ourselves. To miss out on all this would be a mistake."

— Michael Mott

" 'Your body is a bundle of drying wheat,' Denver Butson writes, but not of y<u>our</u> body. From sparks of brushfires, from the physical and psychological burnings, drownings, and suicides in these emotionally audacious poems, Butson himself builds 'a bonfire/of alarm clocks and wristwatches,' of ghazals and elegies and anaphora, with all those who will stay on to celebrate joy, and he and they (and sometimes Lorca, it seems) 'have been dancing in the town-square/since long before dusk.' This is your invitation, reader. You can walk on into your ritual, or strike your imagination on the tinder of these poems."

—Forrest Gander

"When Frost said a poem must be a 'wild tune,' he couldn't have had Denver Butson's poetry in mind, but here is a poet who is wild, frenzied, and refreshingly mad. His imagination unlocks for us the cells of reason and sets us loose in a world of dizzying possibilities."

—Billy Collins

for Rhonda Keyser, still.

Denver Butson's Translations Into Art
—Edmund White

There are extravagant images in these poems, but there are also everyday things—birds, windows—that have been chilled by immersion in the infinite. The extravagance can be evoked by acrobats at the Effigy Café, or by ghosts, goddesses, sacrifices, acts of magic, or by mirages. But the everyday things are haloed by the same crystal ping! of magical language and vision ("swallows slice and reslice the dusk") or of earnest iteration ("it's impossible to live without yearning").

It's as if Denver Butson were weaving his tissue from both burlap and silk, for he sets down the homely facts of a father's and mother's regrets, longings and pains, but he instantly crosses them —elevates them—with the grateful, ennobling language of myth. The mother has a heart condition and has started smoking again (so much for reality), but she is also a dreamer who dreams the house is on fire (her visionary susceptibility); we feel that if she were asked (as Cocteau was asked) what she would save out of a burning house, she would (like Cocteau) respond, "The fire."

"My mother wishes someone/would translate her into a different language," Butson writes—and it is the son who has performed the saving act of finding tightly equivalent meanings in utterly foreign sounds. In the same way the poem "let's move all things" is about loneliness and decay and fire, but poised against so many tropes of evanescence is the word *perfect*, which keeps ringing through the lines like a promising tocsin of eternity. These poems could be inscribed in a missal for mystical atheists.

Butson, like his masters Trakl and Celan, has taught us that "everything that walks in the sun/is a door that could lead somewhere else"—and this sense of immanence reveals to us that this young poet is an "educational" writer, in the root sense of leading his readers out of ignorance and the illusion of fixed identity into the wisdom of flux. As he puts it,

> when you left
> I tried to translate
> everything you left
> into something

In the Middle Ages "to translate" meant to carry or convey to heaven; in this latterday, disillusioned world, the only possible translation is into the heaven of art.

Contents

Magic 15

My Father   My Mother 16

let's move all things 18

If I were the moon . . . 20

What Happens to Fire 21

five o'clock 22

Let's Move All Things 23

from the Brooklyn Refrigerator Magnetic Poetry Series 24

The Last Good Light on Grove Avenue 25

let's move all things (variation 13) 27

Another Street Mirage 28

Textual Marriage ("King . . ." / "Coda") 30

Something in My Ear 31

The Acrobats in the Effigy Café 32

let's move all things (variation 12) 34

Blue in Green 35

Drowning Ghazal (Theodore Roethke) 36

Textual Marriage ("Showmen's . . ." / "Consumed"/ etc.) 37

Here's to your eyes . . . 41

The 1900s 42

Drowning Ghazal (Paul Iluard) 43

Blue in Green 44

If This Weren't a Dream 45

The Fleamarket of the Soul 46

A fisherman hauled the moon from the icy pond 47

at dawn the tourists . . .   48

Textual Marriage ("Prose Poem" / *New York Times*)   49

Drowning Ghazal   50

What They Told Each Other   52

Blue in Green (for Ellis)   54

Blue in Green   55

Before the Turn of the Century   56

November Ordinances   57

today let's forget . . .   58

Every Morning   59

Susquehanna   60

At Main Street Grill in Richmond, Virginia the Waitress Tapped Me on the Shoulder and Said: 61

let's move all things, reprise   62

Hope   63

Blue in Green (for Chris)   64

Drowning Ghazal (John Yau)   65

My Mother My Father   66

Sand Bar   Merriman Nebraska   67

Kiss my Wings . . .   68

Goodbye You   69

You Held Alphabets   70

to dream of birds   71

Blue in Green   72

My Mother My Father   73

Autumn   74

Notes   75

all the black same I dance my blue head off

—John Berryman

Magic

If you take the word *bird*
and reverse the *i* and *r*
and add an *e* to the end
you have *bride*

a bird that has turned into a bride

who with the insertion
of one simple *g*
becomes *bridge*

if you have all three
in flesh not ink
a bird over a bride
on a bridge
you have magic

Magic
which you cannot spell
from the collected letters
of its combined ingredients.

My Father   My Mother

My father is a translation
from a 19th century Russian novel
He is the Papa with big moustaches
a gruff voice and a too-soft heart

My mother is every woman character
in every novel she reads on the backporch
and then tosses into a grocery bag
to take to the old people's home up the road

My father fought the Huns fought the Communists
fought the Nazis fought the Viet Cong
My father still fights the Viet Cong

My mother says *your father still fights them*
and drinks coffee in her nightgown on the backporch
She's started smoking again
despite her heart condition

My father says *listen to this*
and plays a recording of the very old
and broken Billie Holiday
and sits in a chair and fights tears

My mother says *I dream sometimes
that the house is on fire
and when I wake up
I swear I smell smoke*

My father says *she always smells smoke*
He wants to take a cruise around the globe
or at least a weekend in the mountains

My mother wants to sit
on the backporch at night
with a flashlight and shine it
in the startled eyes of skunks
and laugh

My father traps them now
and takes them to a farm up the road
and lets them out sliding the door up
and running back to the truck
He used to shoot them with a pistol
but he locked all his guns up in a safe
after my brother died

My mother wishes someone
would translate her into a different language
a language with no memory of what happened
many years before she could speak it
but she doesn't know what language that would be

My father takes her hand and puts it to his lips

My mother pulls her hand away
tickled by his whiskers

let's move all things
(*when the crow is removed*, variation 42)

Time traced in the bent paths of stars
Something is perfect   must be perfect   is perfect

Girls along the shore
 whisper perfumed wine
 and tongue the war of loneliness

Wars choose the most ancient towns
 to pillage
Even the rain is exiled from cleansing
Time is traced in the bent paths of stars

Something is must be must be perfect

Skeletons get drunk
 on wine and language

Skeletons invade the moon
 with lusty promises

Time traced in bent paths

Blossoms fall on weeping men
Skeletons spend their lives
 as drunk as governors
Something is perfect

Girls along the shore
 with their wine-perfumed breath
 obey the clocks
 wound by tongues
 between their thighs
Their skeletons ache with longing
 that their brains do not understand

                                        must be perfect

Everything is on fire
when the perfumed breath
incites the wind
to mount the tired earth

Time is traced in the bent paths of stars
And everything is perfect   must be   is   perfect

If I
were the
moon I'd
tongue the
dancing stars

If I
were the
stars I'd
lean into
the moon

If I
were myself
I don't
know what

What Happens To Fire

this is fire she says and touches her belly
no this is fire he says and strikes a match

that is a lesser fire she says
a lesser fire than what? he asks
than this she points to her belly *this is fire*

I don't know what you're talking about he says
no you don't know you don't know what I'm talking about
she says

this is fire? he asks touching her belly
I think so she says
yes he says *I think so too*

I'm not sure anymore she says *what is fire*

I used to think this was fire he says and strikes a match
that is fire she says watching the flame
but this isn't he asks and touches her belly

I don't know she says *I don't know what this is*

five o'clock

The air is old
April smells of November
Bells consider tolling
but refrain faintly

Birds fly up
sharp against
the sky
behind them

The hand closes
upon itself
as bony
as five o'clock

Let's Move All Things

everyday sir I saw a man who poked out his own eyes with his thumbs
so he wouldn't have to see too much anymore

I saw specialists with briefcases
waiting for buses their eyes skimming newspapers

I saw those same newspapers later
churning like tumbleweed in the wind

everyday I saw people who looked as if they hadn't danced
since they were babies   lined up at cash machines

I saw a beggar with no legs
walk on his hands for change

I saw men and women staring at red numbers
streaming past on a lighted sign
on the side of a building

everyday

and I don't know about you sir
but I've checked my wrist for a pulse
I've checked my pulse for a heartbeat

I've checked my heartbeat for a reason
to keep on beating

and sir?
the skyline was not enough
the churchbell not enough
the newspaper checkbook   wind-rippled flag
not enough

sir I've seen swallows slice and reslice the dusk
and that's enough
for me to want to keep on seeing

from the Brooklyn Refrigerator Magnetic Poetry Series

you kiss me
lips like fire flowers
naked belly a deep secret
open sex a blushing eternity

my shadow is always drunk
the wind rips through our gowns
lust is a sad goddess screaming

you kiss me

broken ghosts of men
love like animals
the haunted sacrifices
of their wild women

beneath the concrete moon
prisoners of desire
ache for yesterday

The Last Good Light on Grove Avenue
(for Patrick Ryan)

in the last good light of dusk
the news flickers behind glass
a woman with scissors snips away
at her hair in front of a mirror
a car starts but does not back out
of a garage   in the last good light
you can hear the guns one neighborhood over
and you remember the promises you broke
years or maybe just moments
after whispering them into someone's ear
in the last good light of dusk
and one of many men who smoke too fast
and talk to themselves comes out
of a halfway house and calls
a name he thinks is yours
out across the relative silence of going home
and a dog long-conquered
by a newspaper and a stare
whimpers on a porch
all in the last good light
before the East End moon
spills its promise across town
to the ashen regret
of the West End sun
in the last good light
and the street lamps signal
something you know is meant for you—
they signal on   then off   then on again

I don't know if this is drowning or coming up for air

—Michael Ondaatje

let's move all things
(variation 13)

the countryside will suck the countryside dry of sun
what matter if under the round earth
Atlas swears of his aching neck
what matter if horsemen wish for office jobs

the world will dream of dreams
what matter if the soul raises its voice
for a spot in eternity
if the gravedigger wants to lie down on the job
what matter if the sky pulls the bells

if the sun dies   what matter

what matter if the singers scorn the song
what matter if we never remember
all we have forgotten
what matter if our eyes stare out of our heads
like bullet holes
if our birdlike tongues dance
in our mouths
if our shrunken genitals
turn over whenever our names are whispered suddenly

let's fatten the wolves
let's drive the scaffold stakes deep into earth

let's send for a violinist

Another Street Mirage

a man is walking backwards down Seventh Avenue
as if someone has got him by the scruff of his neck
and is pulling him lean along the sidewalk

he is shirtless and wiry
tanned rough above his cowboy jeans
belted low with a fat strap of leather

you think you might see him anywhere else—
at a riverside campsite in the Welfare woods
of Pennsylvania shooting at catfish
with his brother the cop's old .38
fish he'll fry with whole sticks of butter
and pepper so thick the fish's gray
will be lost to black before a night of cheap beer
and a stab at love with his wife
worn dark-eyed from hauling
the kids around all day
while he drinks himself into dulled edges
of what he used to be
in the matter-of-fact light of afternoon

you think you might see him
behind a restaurant
in a Virginia college town
smoking yet another cigarette
down to its nub
and flicking it at a Dumpster
snarling his mantra to nobody in particular
fucking spoiled college kids
whose dishes he washes
when he would rather be riding the rails
even though he knows but won't admit
that his days for riding rails
are behind him   were behind him
before he ever took hold of them

you think you might see him
anywhere else but here
you'd never expect to see him here—
this concrete glare of noon
Monday mid-June Manhattan
against a pastel blot of clustered tourists
among the sharp-healed lunchtime walks
of sallow New Yorkers

not here with his scrawny scarred gut
and muscles like jerked meat
the wound of his mouth nearly hidden
by his pale moustache and beard

not here
scruffed by invisible hands
and dragged backwards down Seventh Avenue

pleading *Easy Officer Easy*
I ain't a bad man

and then disappearing
like so many street mirages
into a crowd about to cross
at the light.

Textual Marriage
("King of Dead Pans Plays Dead Drunk," *Photo*, May 1952
and "Coda" by James Tate)

The band plays "Three o'Clock in the Morning"
Love is not worth so much
and Buster Keaton walks out of the past
I regret everything
into the ring of the Medrano Circus in Paris
Now on our backs in Fayetteville Arkansas
In frozen-faced pantomime
the stars are falling
he acts out his skit
into our cracked eyes
and the French call him "Plus drôle que jamais
with my good arm I reach for the sky
Funnier than ever"
and let the air out of the moon

Something in My Ear
(woven from a Berryman line)

She muttered something
something about her body
in my ear
something about her soul
I've forgotten
something about our wings
to fly us out of here she said
as we danced

She muttered something
something like *the anguish
of the body is silenced by fucking*
in my ear
or *my breasts are closer
to my soul than they are
to my flesh*
I've forgotten
or *our wings cannot be starved
for starvation feeds them*
as we danced.

The Acrobats in the Effigy Café

The acrobats who drink all day in the Effigy Café
won't reveal their ages to just anyone
They let the ashes from their cigarillos fall up
in a magic they won't explain
fall up into the air and weave wreaths
of ash around their acrobats heads

When the acrobats who drink all day in the Effigy Café
reach the edge of drunkenness
they speak of suicides
secretaries they never loved enough
dreams they remembered suddenly in mid-air

And the acrobats who drink all day in the Effigy Café
finish each other's sentences
drink from each other's tumblers
touch indiscriminately under the table

The tiniest piece of lint on the waitress's lip
is enough flint for the acrobats
who drink all day in the Effigy Café
to ignite great monologues about Paris
the misplaced net in Milan
the night the clown died in Tuva

They drink all day in the Effigy Café
and never mention other acrobats
speaking only of dancers dancers and poets

And their eyes fall silent
as if they were there in Granada
when Garcia Lorca was dragged off
to the orchard by fascists
and the acrobats spit out
the word *fascists*

and look away when the waitress
lays the check on the table and undoes her apron
and the night waitress takes her place

Then the acrobats who drank all day
in the Effigy Café leave the check untouched on the table
and excuse themselves to *powder their noses*
rising on uncertain legs
long after the sun has fallen
and the parking lot flickers with failing bulbs.

let's move all things
(variation 12)

the horses will gallop tomorrow
the leaves will trace their dying
  to the sidewalks

don't even think about escaping

the moon has been electrified
  to help direct our search parties

let's look on as the blindmen sell fog
let's eye up the travelers who
  bring their sadnesses to new places
let's watch as the ancient drink
  to the ancient plague of life

let's empty the cellos and accordions
  to find the soul's dropped change

let's colonize the watch and the clock

let's drag our palpitating infinities
  over the jealous beaches

and chant our manifestos
  under suicide bridges

Blue in Green

it's February
but the sky is November gray

a crowd watches a train
from a platform

as if they have emerged
from the stillness of graves

this is one place at one hour
there are so many others
it's impossible to live without yearning

Drowning Ghazal
(with a first line by Theodore Roethke)

Have you come to unhinge my shadow,
come to free, then break, then singe my shadow?

Was that you I saw last night on the lawn?
What did you see? Why did you cringe, My Shadow?

The drowning woman grabbed me by the neck and laughed.
It was enough to start you on another binge, My Shadow.

I found you in the carpet, caught a glimpse of you on the walls,
spotted you on the ceiling and in the curtain's fringe, My Shadow.

Is there any regret, Denver, any urge to rearrange?
Do you feel any guilt, even a tinge, My Shadow?

Textual Marriage

1
("Showmen's League Memorial" and James Tate's "Consumed")

On June 22, 1918 at about 4 AM
why should you believe in magic
the Hagenbeck-Wallace circus train was heading toward Hammond,
Indiana
pretend an interest in astrology
carrying 400 performers and roustabouts
or the tarot?

The train stopped near Ivanhoe
truth is you are free
in order to cool an overheated wheel bearing box
and what might happen to you today
red lights were turned on to warn any other approaching trains
nobody knows
that a train has stopped on the tracks
and your personality may undergo a radical transformation

An empty troop train was approaching
in the next half hour
at full speed from behind
so it goes
piloted by the engineer, Alonzo Sargent
you are consumed
who had previously been fired for sleeping on the job
by your faith in justice

Ignoring the red lights
your hope for a better day
and the efforts of flagmen
the rightness of fate
to signal the oncoming train
the dreams, the lies, the taunts
it plowed into the back of the circus train
nobody gets what he wants
destroying three cars

A dark star passes through you
before finally coming to a halt
on your way home from the grocery
A fire then broke out
never again are you the same

Survivors of the crash
an experience which is impossible to forget
trapped under the wreckage
impossible to share
were unable to free themselves
the longing to be pure is over
and escape the flames

You are the stranger
an estimated 86 people died in the accident
who gets stranger by the hour
most of the dead were never identified.

2
(Billy Collins' "Blues" and "Showmen's League Memorial, 2")

Much of what is said here
circus workers were often known by nicknames
must be said twice
and may had joined only recently
a reminder that no one
two stones for example
takes an immediate interest in anyone
are labeled "Baldy" and "4-Horse Driver"

Nobody will listen it will seem
almost all the others simply read
if you simply admit
"Unknown Male" followed by a number

Your baby left this morning
Hagenbeck-Wallace Circus
she didn't even say goodbye
only missed one show date
but if you sing it again
the one scheduled for Hammond
with the help of a band
by the next day

which will now lift you
they had borrowed enough acts
to a higher more ardent and beseeching key
from other circuses
people will not only listen
to be able to put on the scheduled performances
they will shift to the sympathetic edges of their chairs
in Beloit Wisconsin
moved to such acute anticipation

Five days after the crash
by that chord and the delay that follows
the survivors gathered at Woodlawn Cemetery
they will not be able to sleep
in Chicago
unless you release with one finger
for the burial of 56 fellows
a scream from the throat of your guitar
in a section owned by the Showmen's League of America
and turn your head back to the microphone
bought several months before the crash
to let them know
years later
you're a hard-hearted man

Five elephants were placed at the corners
but that woman's sure going to make you cry
and rear center of the Showmen's Rest Plot

Much of what is said here must be said twice

3
("Showmen's League Memorial, 3" and Weldon Kees' "The Patient is Rallying")

According to local legend
difficult to recall an emotion that is dead
the elephants are there to commemorate the elephants
particularly so among these unbelieved fanfares
killed in the wreck
and admonitions from a camouflaged sky
and buried in this section

I should have remained burdened
in some versions
with distractions

The elephants are said to have aided in rescuing trapped performers
perhaps or stayed drunk
by pulling away burning wreckage
or obeyed the undertaker who was quite charming after all
at the cost of their own lives
or was there a room like that one

It's said that some nights
worn with whispers and
the haunting cries of elephants
a great tree blossoming outside blue windows
can still be heard
warm rain blowing in the night
in the distance
there seems to be some doubt
in reality

No doubt however
there were no elephants on the circus train
of the chilled and empty tissues of the mind
and no animals were killed in the crash

Cold, cold, a gray winter entering
most of the left half of the Showmen's plot
like spines of air
contains victims
frozen in an ice cube
of the 1918 wreck

Here's
to
your
eyes
that
smell
of
disappearing
and
here's
to
my
fatal
drunkenness

The 1900s

there was a sky
once
so blue it deafened you

there was an opening hand
and a white bird
blooming

there was your belly

and my lips across
your belly

there was a tiny radio
on a kitchen counter

and music

there was music
we could barely hear

but somehow managed
to dance to

Drowning Ghazal
(with a first line by Paul Iluard)

And your thirst to be naked extinguishes all nights
your thirst to dissolve exterminates all nights

I have forgotten my own name in the presence of your loins
et ta soif d'jtre nue iteint toutes les nuits

and drowned in the illegible handwriting of your eyelashes
I have lost distinction between this and all nights

you dreamt of fire of mirrors of tongues
after days with you I slept hungrily all nights

there will be nothing left of us one day but sin
sin and what your nakedness did to me all night

Blue in Green

sometimes I remember the night
the moon burned and everything else

I saw it above the strain of our city
burning

how I touched your neck
and it too was burning

sometimes I stand on the bridge
between here and there
I look out
as unknowing boats
pass beneath me

I could drop onto one of them I think
make my presence known

but I prefer the anonymity
of this nostalgic pose

a man trembling in an overcoat
under a cold moon

If This Weren't a Dream

In a dream
I'm playing
a busted accordion

and you're trying
to learn that trick
where a white bird
suddenly flies out
of your palm

if this weren't
a dream
I would tell you
you need to have
the bird first
in order
for the trick
to work

and you'd tell me
to get my accordion fixed
if I'm going to make
such a racket with it

if this weren't a dream
we would both bust up
laughing at the word *racket*

and a white bird
would fly suddenly
out of your mouth

The Fleamarket of the Soul

I'll give you a horse galloping through fire
for five dead crows at the feet of a blindman

I'll give you the charred trees at the edge of the abyss
for the snarl of a dog about to break its leash

I'll give you a wedding ring over swollen flesh
for an appetite for love

I'll give you what usually happens when I'm drunk
for the clarity that follows a hangover

I'll give you eternity for one guiltless dusk
ten thousand dreams for one thing unbroken by memory

I'll give you the wings of angels' blades
for the dancing girls of ribcages

flesh steaming from a bath
for teeth bloodied by wine

I'll give you a bird's nest
for the ripe flesh of your loins

I'll give you wind and silence
for your breath and voice

I'll give you the hollow inside a clock's guts
for the strength to multiply zero by infinity

I'll give you my shadow's passport
for the walking shoes of my forgetfulness

A fisherman hauled the moon from the icy pond
(from a line by Georg Trakl)

A fisherman hauled the moon
  from the icy pond

nearby birds turned into angels
  and angels turned on the sun

a fisherman hauled the moon

shepherds in the forest
  forgot to extinguish the sun

a naked youth appeared
  and watched the corruption
  of flowers and stars

a fisherman hauled the moon from the icy pond

at
dawn
the
tourists
expect
Van Gogh
or
perhaps
Liberace
to
enter
their
sad
dreams

Textual Marriage
(James Tate's "Prose Poem" and a news article from the New York Times)

I am surrounded by the pieces of this large puzzle
a man has been accused of fatally stabbing his bride
here's a piece I call my wife
at a post-reception party
and here's an odd one I call convictions
just 10 hours after they exchanged wedding vows
here's conventions here's collisions
at 11:00 PM on Saturday
conflagrations congratulations
the newlyweds and about fifteen members of their wedding party
such a puzzle is this
went to the bride's apartment
I like to grease up all the pieces
partygoers said the couple and other people were drinking heavily
and pile them in the center of the basement

Drowning Ghazal

Sometimes they would remember the birds
She had dreams that they dismembered the birds

Summers she worried about the dog overheating
Autumns she fed squirrels and all through December the birds

Before the fire his biggest fear was drowning
After the fire he searched the embers for birds

She said it was *more impossible to breathe than to fly*
He said *let's name this time our "September of Birds"*

I could hear her talking all through my sleep
She pointed at the sky and whispered *Denver the birds*

A list of my nightmares
is the way out of here

—Anne Carson

What They Told Each Other

he told her he owned
an acre of moon dust
that they could go there sometime

that he had a small farm
he kept in a box
under his bed

he said he had been watching her lips
for years since five o'clock

that her neck reminded him
of someone else's memory

that her voice took him back
to a place he had never been

he said *your breasts are like
burning ice cubes*

and I mean that as a compliment
he said

he told her that her belly was a reflection of sky
in a cup of coffee

he said *may I sit next to you
while you dance?*

she told him that the cello
always made her think of a single bird
across a November sky

she said she had been counting backwards
since as long as she could remember

she said *when I see other women
I want to lie with them
like a man lies with them
and I want to never stop lying with them*

but she said *it's not what you're thinking*
I still ache for men ache for you really
the way evening aches for dark

she said she could tell by the way he walked
that he had drowned once in a former life

that this life for him
was a process of undrowning

she whispered *out there*
in the faraway rooms of train cries
is my soul

in here she said
right in here
I am nothing but thirst
and hunger

she said *yes you may sit next to me*
while I dance.

Blue in Green
(for Ellis)

the sun is a creep
who never shows his face
around here
anymore

I am aristocratic
in my sordidness

the bridge out there
is the only hypnosis
I need

the trumpet bares its teeth
and then returns to silence

silence
the movement of cars
against a distant horizon

I report to you
from the other side
of the world

Blue in Green

rain   traffic
day's slow pouring in
lamps lit despite clocks

the sky over the bridge whispers
a bird's thin rising
slice of smoke from a chimney

Before the Turn of the Century

I remember telling you about the birds
they way they exploded
like applause

and the time you taught me the word *ennui*
how to keep my tongue out of the way
when saying it

I remember your beautiful apologies
especially the ones I didn't deserve

but most of all
I remember the afternoons
how we spent them
watching the secondhand
escort the calendar off the page

November Ordinances

who sets the town clock
is afraid of the dark

who rounds up the rats
has an illegible address

who says *the wind is asleep*
you are alone where is your shadow?
says it into the skin of your neck

who fires the furnaces
owns the dusk

who puts a bullet in her head
in the forest where the highway ends
is forgiven her infidelities
by the next generation

who says *day doesn't break it shatters*
is always drunk when night falls

today
let's
forget
to
remember
how
slain
our
hearts
will
be
when
it's
over

Every Morning

every morning time begins again
the city grows out of the swamp
new bridges span new rivers
birds twist themselves out of the sky's nothing

every morning cafés rise tables sprout
and patrons drink their first coffees
and turn pages of newspapers
which have miraculously appeared in their hands
reading news of things that happened yesterday
before the world was made

every morning a man grows out of a doorway
and stands on the sidewalk
next to the first trashbin of the new world
he wipes his hands on his apron
and squints into the sun
having just discovered meat
and invented the art of butchery

Susquehanna

Just out of reach
of the exhausted breath
of factory towns

the skittish boys giggle
with rocks
in their palms

When the train comes
they will throw them
and duck
sparks clacking up

Across the tracks
and down a grassy hill
the slow river turns
over the bones
of years

The boys are men now
drunk and pissing
crouching to find
just the right rock
to palm
and throw again

At Main Street Grill in Richmond, Virginia
The Waitress Tapped Me on the Shoulder and Said:

when you are done eating Honey
you're going to leave this restaurant
and walk across the street and when you
get to the other side you'll turn around
and realize that this place is gone
because it is this place is nowhere
it's not here it's just a dream

and you'll swear that seconds before
you were eating in here
that you smiled at the waitress
who poured you more water
and told you it was all just a dream

and you'll know then that I was right
and you'll stand there looking across the street
at this empty space
where you swear there was once a restaurant
where you even thought that moments ago
you were eating

let's move all things, reprise

everyday sir etc.
a dog barks
at the dissolving moon

a city undresses for sleep
and the history of absence
scribbles its laws
around her eyes

so what if nobody notices
what's invisible anymore

so what if everyday sir
is touched by instruments
and recorded in ledgers

sir beneath the sidewalks
there are trembling serpents
seething with briefcases

there's a hinge on a door
about to snap off in the wind

everyday there's a skyline
growing a little smaller
in her imagination
everyday sir etcetera

Hope
(for cnc)

you keep believing the highway's scattered alphabets
will spell something that makes sense
they always do eventually

a woman's voice in your ear once did
but she is no longer there

you remember little things
a stray hair across her face
the way she started and restarted her sentences

once you drove with her across the desert
ocean of sky opium blue
her lips trying to find the words
to the country song on the radio

but that was September
many lives ago

the crows at that road carcass up ahead
you know will startle up
when your car passes

but they will be back at the carcass again
before leaving the sight of your rearview

and this alone
gives you hope

Blue in Green
(for Chris)

our anguish is of course
the light through the glass
on the window sill

everything that walks in the sun
is a door that could lead us somewhere else
if we let it

sometimes our houses stand
and sometimes they fall

the direction of the wind
has very little to do with it

sometimes we surrender
and sometimes we put our hands
in our pockets
and keep on not fighting

Drowning Ghazal
(first line by John Yau)

Once I was as tender as a broken wing
I thought my likeness should be rendered as a broken wing

She stood still under the ashtray sky
She posed on the fender as a broken wing

There was something about drowning in the throat of a train
I saw myself at the end of a bender as a broken wing

It had more to do with the curve of her lips
her eyes as slender as a broken wing

She said she couldn't place me in the mess of her past
and later *I see you Denver as a broken wing.*

My Mother My Father

My mother opens a door
and spies on herself
as a much younger woman

I was so happy then she thinks
*with those boots   that skirt
and look at my hair
I was so happy then*

My father opens a door
and spies on himself
as a much younger man

look how happy I was then
he thinks *with a big fast car
and no nightmares of war*

My mother and father open a door
and spy on themselves
as a much younger couple

we must have been happy then
they think *with music we liked
on the radio and no telephone
rattling death's dice
in the cold fist of the night*

Sand Bar Merriman Nebraska

after the unquiet highways
are conquered into dust

after the wind's eyes have yellowed
and the sky has lain its longing down
in its boneless grave

after the sun is spoken of only in past tense
if spoken of at all
as history   memory

after thunder no longer deafens you
and dreams stop blinding you
of sleep

will you follow me here
and will you smooth back my hair
like you once did

when we were young
when we had just run through rain
and sat shivering on your porch?

Kiss my
wings you
told me

I kissed
them and
you said
Kiss my
shadow so
I kissed
your shadow

What will
I do
when you
leave me?

Goodbye You
(for rjk)

Goodbye to you now
you who issued kisses
to my lower and upper halves
you who called the cows home
to roost in the high trees
of my saddest thoughts
you who called me wind
and said *blow my dress off*
you who chased away my disgust
my despair my disrepair goodbye
you whose secret freckles
I have discovered and charted
on the maps for the ages
you who allowed me
to be the cartographer
of your terrain
goodbye
you whose maps
I made
and studied
and revised
upon second and third
and three thousandth expedition
goodbye
you whose seas
I can't imagine another sailing
whose forests I can't imagine
another traipsing
whose freckles
I can't imagine another contemplating
goodbye
I'll be right back
I'm just going to get some wine.

You Held Alphabets

in your perfect palms

you said you could teach me
a thing or two
about silence

you made tiny bouquets
of tiny flowers

and set them aflame
in my dreams

when you left
I tried to translate
everything you left
into something

this is the best I could do
a fingerprint smeared
on a tilted-back glass

to dream of birds

    birds. ricocheting
    off the cement grey sky.

        to dream of birds
        in the unswept
        pathways of morning.

    the shrapnel edges
    of birds' wings.

        to dream of them.
        the gunpowder shadows
        of flown birds

Blue in Green

and the shadow of a bird
crosses the floor
but by the time you look
through the window
the bird is gone

nothing that can be written
anymore
has already been written

all we can do is not unwrite
what has not yet been unwritten

night is delivered like a telegram
and recited like a telegram
with all the stops

weeks go by in one moment

outside   the curious baggage of our lives
waits for trains   without us

so much that is inside those bags
will never see the light
of this or any other day

My Mother My Father

My mother says
*that's the corner I was on
when I met your father*

My father was a hoodlum
with a convertible
and a cigarette

My mother had a scarf in her hair
and a wad of gum in her mouth
She was a farm girl in the city for the day

My father was wearing dungarees
My mother had on pedal pushers
like the girls wore in the magazines

They each dated the other's friend
and then tired of them
and dated each other
kissed on country roads
got married
had four boys
lost one to a bullet
and wished
for more grandchildren

My father's trousers sag now at the waist
My mother's slacks are always pressed

My mother and father sit on the backporch
The stars race across the sky
like years

Autumn
(after Paul Celan)

It's an effort now
to beat the heart
an effort to inflate the lungs

long ago we embraced
under the moon's absent gaze

we slept like wine
in forgotten bottles

we spoke truths
into each other's palms
and threw the spoken
truths to the wind

and now it's Autumn
as if time has a right
to keep moving forward

Notes

the "let's move all things" poems are from a series of poems generated from various texts, particularly the poems of Vicente Huidobro.

James Tate's "Coda" quoted almost in its entirety in "Textual Marriage" was originally published in *The Oblivion Ha-Ha* (Atlantic-Little, Brown).

The line "she muttered something in my ear I've forgotten as we danced" is from John Berryman's poem "Her and It" from his *Love and Fame*, as reprinted in *The Collected Poems 1937-1971* (Noonday).

The "Blue in Green" poems are all inspired by repeated listenings to Bill Evans' composition of the same title on Miles Davis' *Kind of Blue* (Columbia Records).

Theodore Roethke's line "Have you come to unhinge my shadow?" is from his poem "The Shape of the Fire" as printed in *The Collected Poems* (Anchor Books).

"Showman's League Memorial" is from a website detailing the 1918 circus train wreck.

James Tate's "Consumed" appears in his book *The Oblivion Ha-Ha* (Atlantic-Little, Brown).

Billy Collins' "Blues" appears in his book, *The Art of Drowning* (University of Pittsburgh Press).

Weldon Kees' "The Patient is Rallying" is from his *Collected Poems* (University of Nebraska Press).

Paul Iluard's line "et ta soif d'jtre nue iteint toutes les nuits" appears here in French and as translated into English by Marilyn Kallet as it appears in *The Last Love Poems of Paul Iluard* (Louisiana).

"A fisherman hauled the moon from the icy pond" is Robert Firmage's translation of a line in Georg Trakl's "Rest and Silence" in *Song of the West* (North Point Press).

"What Happens to Fire" has been made into a short film directed by Kevin Doyle and starring Rhonda Keyser, Matt Ellis, and Denver Butson.

James Tate's "Prose Poem" appears in *The Oblivion Ha-Ha* (Atlantic-Little, Brown).

John Yau's line "Once I was as tender as a broken wing" is from his poem "Radiant Silhouette V" published in *Radiant Silhouette* (Black Sparrow Press).

The text of "At Main Street Grill . . ." is what a waitress said to me, word-for-word, as best as I can remember it when I wrote it down a few minutes later in my notebook.

The Sand Bar is a bar in Merriman, Nebraska. Cedric Chatterley titled this poem, before I had the pleasure of visiting the Sand Bar myself.

DENVER BUTSON's first book of poetry, *triptych*, appeared on The Commoner Press in 1999. His poems have also been published in *The Yale Review*, *The Ontario Review*, *Quarterly West*, *Caliban*, *Exquisite Corpse*, and *Cairn*, among other journals. In fall 1999, he was the first Ronald H. Bayes Writer in Residence at St. Andrews Presbyterian College. He teaches privately for his own writers' studio, WritersWriting, in New York City.